TOMORROW CAN WAIT...

YESTERDAY IS PAST...

LIVE TODAY!

TOMORROW CAN WAIT...

YESTERDAY IS PAST...

LIVE TODAY!

The Art of Living in Tranquility

JIM COLLEY

**All scripture, unless otherwise noted,
will be from the King James Version,
The New Living Translation,
or The Amplified Bible**

ISBN: 1492242748
ISBN 13: 9781492242741
Library of Congress Control Number:
2013915579
CreateSpace Independent Publishing Platform
North Charleston, South Carolina

Table of Contents

Dedication and Acknowledgments

I would first like to thank the One who radically changed my life forty-two years ago: Jesus Christ. The new identity I received from being in him has truly made me a man who is deeply loved, greatly blessed, and highly favored.

I would then like to thank the love of my life, my wife Melanie, who for thirty-four years has faithfully helped and supported our ministry, and without whom this book would not have been possible.

I would like to say thank you to my wonderful children, Lindsay, Jessica, Kristen, and Lauren and our son-in-law, Brent, who have taught me the joys of being a parent.

I would like to say how blessed I am to have three terrific grandchildren, Kaden, Kolby, and Kalea. Just thinking about them brings a smile to my face.

Finally, I would like to say thank you to the Family Worship Center, the members of which have believed in me, my leadership, and the principles on which this book expounds.

Prologue

Why I Wrote This Book

All of my Christian life, I had a God who was packaged away, nicely and neatly, in a little box that I thought I could understand. I had "formulas" from the Bible for every problem and relationship that could possibly come up. There were formulas for child-rearing, dating, marriage, employer/employee relationships, political stances, health and healing, and more. I was taught from my youth up that there is a certain "group" I needed to stay in for answers in life, and it would be "unsafe" to venture outside of this group for advice and answers to life's problems. My life was a neat little package in which I also found my God—"inside the box."

Then approximately two and a half years ago, while browsing at a local bookstore, I came across a book by Eckhart Tolle entitled,

The Power of Now. At first, I merely read the book with interest in what was being said.

While I had heard the teachings of Jesus and of the Apostle Paul since I was a child, suddenly an unbelievable enlightenment was taking place through the words of this book. I then decided to reread the book, this time cross-referencing it with the Bible. I began devouring each word and phrase. This led me to buy some DVDs and CDs by Eckhart Tolle. Even now as I drive, I listen to the CDs. After two and a half years, I have not tired of them. I also realized that other books I was reading, such as *Jesus Calling* by Sarah Young and *The Practice of the Presence of God* by Brother Lawrence, were teaching the same concepts.

Needless to say, a deep transformation took place through these truths and revolutionized my way of thinking—or maybe I should say of "not thinking."

Because all truth comes from God, my life was so changed. I wanted my children, friends, and parishioners to understand and *be able to practice* this beautiful life of peace and joy about which Jesus and Paul spoke.

You see, I now know why Jesus said, *Take no thought for the morrow*[1] (referring to the psychological past). I know why he said, *He that puts his hand to the plough and looks back is not fit for the Kingdom of God*[2] (referring to the psychological future). I know now why Paul said, *Behold now is the accepted time, behold now is the day of salvation*[3] (referring to the power of the present moment). I now know why David said, *This is the day that the Lord has made. We shall rejoice and be glad in it,*[4] (referring to the power of the present moment). I know now why Paul could say from a Roman prison, *Rejoice in the Lord always and again I say rejoice,*[5] (referring to separating life from life situations). I know why he could say from prison, *The peace of God that passes all understanding shall keep your hearts and minds*[6] (again, referring to separating life from life situations). I know why Jesus said, *This joy no man can take from you*[7] (meaning that we need not allow people to steal our joy; to decide how we identify ourselves; or to label us, etc.).

I try now to emphasize to my congregation the importance of obtaining our identity from God and not from others, not even from ourselves. Since my "enlightenment," what Jesus says about me *jumps* from the pages of the Bible in a new and beautiful way. I know now that I am loved, I am accepted, I am forgiven, I am complete, and I am what God says I am. And so are you.

This may be "outside your box," but I ask you not to "throw the baby out with the bath water." May you open your mind to old truths set in a "different" sort of way.

Gandhi said, "Don't let anyone walk through your mind with dirty feet." [8] It's time for those of us who want true peace and joy to be able to listen to someone's beliefs which aren't exactly like ours; to stop slandering, criticizing, and being negative (walking with dirty feet), because many life-changing truths are the same in other religions.

You know, Jesus's teachings can't help us if we produce hate just because all of our beliefs don't line up with those of others. How many wars have been fought in the name of religion and God? How many innocent men, women, and children have been killed because someone said, "God told me to do this"?

You've heard it said: "There are two subjects you shouldn't talk about at the dinner table, religion and politics." Why is this so?

Because religion and politics house our strongest and most adamant belief systems. This has been proven throughout history. Because of differing political views, assassinations and wars have taken place even within our own nation. A classic example of this is the Civil War. What atrocities took place in the 1800's because part of our nation believed differently than the other part. Brother killing brother. All because of a belief system so strong that we felt it was necessary to take life.

Obviously, on the religious level, crucifixions, burnings at the stake, and yes, again, even wars have taken place because of differing religious beliefs. I think about the time of the Crusades and how people who claimed to be religious could kill and massacre men, women, and children.

It's time to realize that the people are not the enemy. Even another's belief system is not the enemy. There is a darker force at work, deceiving people into thinking they are actually doing right by hating and killing others.

Verbal attacks, slander, etc. come from ego—the misguided thought that one has a corner on "the right belief system."

On a larger scale, this hatred may turn into something harmful to humanity by causing people to think that they are doing the world a favor by ridding the earth of certain people. Whether on a small scale or a large scale, all hatred is ego-driven.

If we are going to entertain a judgmental attitude on the thought level, which leads to negativism on the emotional level, our hearts will not be open to this perpetual peace and joy that I'm speaking of in this book.

Most of our belief systems are handed to us by our parents, churches and other people. We have what is called *a conditioned mind*. If I were to ask you, "Why do you have a belief system and what is its purpose?" What would your answer be? Shouldn't it be to help you navigate life? To help you seek the best paths that will take you to the destination you want?

The ultimate destination for all of us would probably be peace, joy, and love. It really doesn't matter what I accomplish if I'm not joyful, peaceful, and loving. Does climbing the corporate ladder or gaining possessions really bring joy anyway?

I submit to you that if our belief system is causing us to be unkind in words and deeds, we need an overhaul. It is damaging our homes, churches and yes, even our nation.

Consider this: First, the Bible says that *God is love* in I John 4:8. His nature is love, kindness, grace, mercy, and forgiveness. Not hatred and murder. As a matter of fact, those are characteristics of Satan, according to John 8:44.

Secondly, when Jesus wanted to teach us about who our neighbor is, he gave us an example of someone who would have held beliefs different from his: a Samaritan.

Look at Luke 10:30-37. Jesus replied with a story: *"A Jewish man was traveling from Jerusalem down to Jericho, and he was attacked by bandits. They stripped him of his clothes, beat him up, and left him half dead beside the road. By chance a priest came along. But when he saw the man lying there, he crossed to the other side of the road and passed him by. A temple assistant walked over and looked at him lying there, but he also passed by on the other side. Then a despised Samaritan came along, and when he saw the man, he felt compassion for him. Going over to him, the Samaritan soothed his wounds with olive oil and wine and bandaged them. Then he put the man on his own donkey and took him to an inn, where he took care of him. The next day he handed the innkeeper two silver coins telling him, 'Take care of this man. If his bill runs higher than this, I'll pay you the next time I'm here. Now which of these three would you say was a neighbor to the man who was attacked by bandits?" Jesus asked.*

The man replied, "The one who showed him mercy."

Then Jesus said, "Yes, now go and do the same."

The religious men (a priest and a temple assistant) walked by the injured man. These men should have understood the teachings of Jesus the most. A non-Jew (a Samaritan) was the one, whom Jesus pointed out, was willing to help.

I think about some difficult times in our nation, and how during these times we set aside our belief systems in order to show compassion. The planes crashing into the Twin Towers in New York City is a prime example. When this event took place, I didn't hear of one incident during the rescue operation when the rescue worker stopped and said, "Now before I rescue you, I need to know what your religious or political beliefs are." That would be absurd to even think about. There were just people trying to help people. Belief systems were set aside. They didn't matter at that time.

So what is wrong with living that way all the time when it comes to showing kindness, love, and compassion? Why shouldn't our words show the type of love that Jesus expressed while he was on earth, all of the time, instead of just during a crisis? My friend, we have to *want* peace and joy, and be willing to pursue the things that *make* for peace and joy, or they will elude us.

Jesus gave his disciples this admonition in Luke 10:5–6: *Whenever you enter someone's home, first say, 'May God's peace be on this house.' If those who live there are peaceful, the blessing will stand; if they are not, the blessing will return to you.*

Wow! We must *desire* peace and joy. No amount of hearing or reading will benefit us if willingness isn't already there. We can't be ego-driven and be after peace and joy at the same time. They are not compatible.

I have such a desire for other people to understand this. While I realize the time has to be right, may this book be an inspiration to all who really need it. If for no other reason, I'm writing this book for my family. I am also writing to show Christians that they don't have to be afraid to hear valuable truths taught by a different source if this source resonates with them in biblical soundness.

May God work in your life, just as he is profoundly working in mine.

Introduction

I Don't Believe in
"If" or "Wish" Anymore

I must start by saying that I am by no means speaking about a life that has been horrible. Yes, I grew up in a broken home. My single mother raised my five siblings and me on welfare and food stamps. Dad left home when I was nine years old and never saw the need to provide alimony or child support, and believe me, we kids paid for it. So did Mom. My negative attitudes were formed early.

However, because of an encounter with God when I was thirteen, I pursued a different way of life than the way in which I was raised. I went off to a Christian college, earned a BS in pastoral theology, and married my high school sweetheart. Together we started a ministry, a family, and a life that would far exceed my wildest dreams. We are now pastoring in the Northeast, have a beautiful house, and four wonderful daughters, a fantastic son-in-law, and three beautiful grandchildren. Things are great!

Something happened, however, a little over two years ago that caused an "awakening." This awakening made me realize that I was not practicing everything I'd learned about Christianity over the past forty years. The "victorious Christian life" that I'd spoken about so many times had eluded me more often than I cared to admit. Oh yes, I'd had my mountaintop experiences like everyone else, but I came to the conclusion that my life didn't show the constant victory I was supposed to have. My emotions were up and down continuously. Most of it had to do with my circumstances or my life situation. If things were going well, I was an amiable person. If things went south, God help my wife, children, or anybody else who received the effect of my loss of joy due to circumstances.

This book is about what I have discovered. Before now, I would've said, "If I had only come upon this years ago," or "I wish I had had this 'awakening' when I was twenty."

But I don't believe in "if" anymore, nor do I "wish." This is a small part of *why* I now have joy and peace in my life that will never leave.

May God enlighten your mind as you read this book, and may a real awakening take place in you. You'll know if it has by the consistent peace and joy you will have within. The joy will not be based on your current circumstances but rather on who you are right now and forever! Enjoy!

Chapter One

Redefining Your Life

*Forget about your life situation and pay attention
to your life. Your life situation exists in time.
Your life is now. Your life situation is mind-stuff.
Your life is real.*
--ECKHART TOLLE, *The Power of Now*

In order for real transformation to take place,
there must be a redefining of that which is
important to you.

In Romans 12:2, Paul says, *Do not be conformed to this world but be transformed by the renew-
ing of your mind.* The word "conformed" means
to take the shape or the mold of something.
In other words, we are not to mold ourselves
to the world's ideas. We are not to be molded
into who the world says we are. We are not to
take the shape of culture. Right now, culture

is definitely caught up in "being happy," and people have some strange ways of trying to achieve it.

On the other hand, "transformed" comes from the same root word from which we get our word "metamorphosis" (as in what happens to a caterpillar when it becomes a butterfly).

A butterfly doesn't conform, it transforms. This change takes place from the inside out. It becomes a new creature, a new creation. It is not a caterpillar anymore. It has a whole new identity. It is a butterfly. We never hear anyone say, "Oh! Look at that flying caterpillar!" Conformity takes place on the outside. True transformation can only take place on the inside. Happiness is an "outside product" caused by circumstances. Joy is an "inside product" that has nothing at all to do with circumstances.

Paul and Silas's imprisonment is a classic example. The Bible says these men had many stripes laid upon them. They were beaten severely. Acts 16:25 goes on to say that after they had been put in the deepest part of the prison, they began to sing praises unto God. What? You've got to be kidding me! They had just been beaten unjustly. Talk about transcending a situation! Talk about taking the worst of all circumstances and going beyond understanding.

This response is not taught in society today. Instead, we blame—circumstances, people, whoever, or whatever is around. After all, it's not my fault that I'm in this dreadful situation! Or we find someone's shoulder to cry on and then go to the doctor and get some pills that will "help" our depression. We are angry because we have been dealt a bad hand in life. Transcending our circumstances by going deep into our being is not something that comes to mind as a way to handle adversity.

Unless, of course, you have concluded that there is someone bigger in this life than you are; someone who is bigger than the person or circumstance that hurt you; someone who is bigger than life, period!

What is it that society, peers, television, culture, and yes, even sometimes family, have told you that you must have? Yes, happiness. That's how fairy tales end—how all good stories end: happily ever after.

The question is, "What is true happiness?" And then, "How do I get there from here?"

A person does not become happy because of anything he or she achieves. True happiness (joy) comes from understanding who you are at the core of your being.

I would like to differentiate between happiness and joy. Joy is a concept that Paul wrote about from a Roman dungeon when he said, *Rejoice in the Lord always, and again I say rejoice* (Philippians 4:4). How can a person have the power to write about joy when he is sitting in prison not knowing whether he will live or die? There must be someone bigger than he or the circumstances in his life, or it just won't happen!

Throughout life, things will happen over which we have no control. If you are after happiness, it will elude you because happiness is circumstantial. It's influenced by outside events or happenings. Joy, on the other hand, does not require things or circumstances to be right. The joy that Jesus said he had was *a joy that no man can take from you* (John 16:22).

If we are honest with ourselves, our lives are an emotional roller coaster, for the most part.

If things are going our way financially, we're happy. If we are struggling financially, we're depressed. If our marriage is going well, we're happy. If our marriage is in turmoil, we're upset. If the stock market is soaring, we are elated. If we're in a recession, we are full of worry and anxiety.

Joy, true joy, will never be determined by what *happens* to you. It is determined by what is going on *inside* you, a place so holy and sacred that no man or circumstance can touch it.

∫

A person can very well be joyful and at peace when he has something deeper than a "surface" life. A person's life has been described as a deep lake. We are the lake. The surface of the lake is what *happens* to us. The storms may rage on the surface, but in the depths of our life, there is peace. This was the reason Paul could write from prison: *and the peace of God which passes all understanding shall keep your hearts and minds through Christ Jesus.*[9] This verse is about transcending circumstances. Transcending people. Transcending the world, period. The word "transcend" means to "go beyond, to surpass." There is only one way to do this. Have something going on inside of you that is so powerful that nothing and no one can touch it.

You see, God is in the "depths" of us. He is the One who causes us to *rejoice in the Lord always.*[10] He is the One who causes the peace to be there. The Bible says that people won't even be able to understand why you can be at peace. Though we mourn, we can be at peace even through tragic death. Though the world reels in financial crisis, we can have a peace more stable than money. Though someone intentionally tries to hurt us, we can live with peaceful hearts and good consciences because vengeance (an outside event) is not in our hearts. Instead, the Spirit is producing love, joy, peace, long-suffering, gentleness, goodness, faith, meekness, and temperance. As these "fruits" are produced in you, you will be able to overcome any obstacle in your life.

What happens to you cannot affect the real you if you don't want it to. The real you happens to be the spirit that God has put in you, made alive to all that is beautiful. Also, you are dead to the influences of the outside world. When Paul said, "I die daily," he wasn't saying that he would no longer have feelings, get hungry, or have desires. He was just saying that desires would no longer control him. The present moment, which is so powerful, allows you to be totally satisfied in God, and to "crucify" each moment as it passes. You don't need the past.

This matter of crucifying every moment that passes cannot wait. It must be done now. Your very joy and peace depend on it!

Most of the time, a past moment that is kept in the present will cause you a world of trouble. Most of our problems and vices are caused by allowing moments to "linger" in our lives. So many times, we hear people say, "It's time to move on with life." What does that really mean? Maybe it's time to stop lingering on what has happened? It's time to let certain thoughts go? You have to ask yourself this question: "Is this thought that I am holding onto helping me in the present moment? Is it encouraging me or discouraging me? Is it making me better or bitter?"

The reason it is so difficult to forgive someone is that we take a *past* word or action and hang on to it in the *present* moment. If you really want to forgive someone, you have to crucify the past in your life. Unresolved conflicts from the past cause bitterness. We refuse to let go of an offense, which leads to unforgiveness. Hanging on to unforgiveness then leads to bitterness. Paul says in Hebrews 12:15 that bitterness always affects other people. The people you work with, the people in your family or church, the people you love the most, will get hurt—all because you refuse to crucify the past.

So, I challenge you to redefine joy and happiness. Define yourself in terms of who you really are rather than in terms of what has happened to you. Redefine what true peace is and the path you will take to have joy and peace. Our minds have to be renewed. We have to take on a new identity. Are you ready for it to happen? Do it now, in the present moment. This can't wait.

Chapter Two

Literally Killing Time

Time is seen as the endless succession of moments, some "good," some "bad." Yet, if you look more closely, that is, through your immediate experience, you'll find that there are not many moments at all. You discover that there only ever is this moment. Life is always now.
--ECKHART TOLLE, *Practicing the Power of Now*

One Valentine's Day, I asked my wife for the book, *The Power of Now* by Eckhart Tolle. It was one of the greatest blessings I have ever received. He was the first person to open my eyes to the fact that time is an *illusion*. After devouring that book, and then going back through it two or three times and underlining many things, I realized that he was teaching many truths that Jesus taught. I had heard these truths my whole life but for some reason

or another, I just never got it. I don't know if
this has ever happened to you, but all of a sud-
den, the light was turned on and it made sense!
I felt so light and joyous. Truly, the peace that
passes understanding entered my soul in a
fresh way!

My purpose is to tell others what happened
in my life. This is exciting stuff! My prayer is
that others will find this peace and joy that
never has to leave, just as I have.

∫

Time truly does equal pain. If you want the pain to
stop, you have to realize the preciousness of the only
moment available: right now. This is great because the
ability to get things done comes from the ability to
focus on the now.

∫

We are told in the Bible that we are to
redeem the time.[11] When Paul made this statement, he wasn't talking about the past or the
future. We know this because it's impossible
to redeem that which has already happened or

to redeem that which hasn't happened yet. The Bible would never ask you to do that which is impossible. The Apostle Paul gives this command to the Ephesians right before he tells them to be filled with the Spirit. One of the main actions of the Holy Spirit is to produce joy and peace in a person's life. Again, Paul, writing to the Galatians, says that *the fruit of the Spirit is love, joy, and peace...*[12]

If we are doing things right and being our most productive, we should also be experiencing the most peace and joy. To *redeem* means to buy back. It is the command to "make the most of each moment." You can't do that if you are constantly living in the past or in the future. As a matter of fact, I have found that some thoughts are great robbers of the present moment.

One is fretting about what happened in the past, which causes me to lose focus on the present. The second robber is worrying about the future, which also causes me to take my eyes off the present. Both cause me to lose focus on the present, which causes the loss of joy and peace. I have found the fruits of the past (guilt, bitterness, anger, depression, etc.) and the fruits of the future (worry, anxiety, etc.) always cause the joy and the peace to leave. It is impossible for joy and peace to cohabit with depression, bitterness, worry, etc. One will cause the other to leave. They won't both stay. You probably have already chosen which fruits should stay. So now, it's time to chase the others away! This is done with a focus on *intense presence*.

∫

Intense presence will take place when you realize that the only time you should allow a past or future event into the present moment is to help you with what you are doing in the present moment. If it doesn't help now, leave it alone. You don't need it.

∫

The helpful past will always work as a guidepost (not as a whipping post or a hitching post), helping you to avoid the same mistakes you made before. It also allows you to see what worked or didn't work in a certain situation. But this information will only be used to help you in the present.

Let's consider Luke 7:36–46: *One of the Pharisees asked Jesus to have dinner with him, so Jesus went to his home and sat down to eat. When a certain immoral woman from that city heard he was eating there, she brought a beautiful alabaster jar filled with expensive perfume. Then she knelt behind him at his feet, weeping. Her tears fell on his feet, and she wiped them off with her hair. Then she kept kissing his feet and putting perfume on them.*

When the Pharisee who had invited him saw this, he said to himself, "If this man were a prophet, he would know what kind of woman is touching him. She's a sinner!" Then Jesus answered his thoughts. "Simon," he said to the Pharisee, "I have something to say to you."

"Go ahead, Teacher," Simon replied.

Then Jesus told him this story: "A man loaned money to two people—500 pieces of silver to one and 50 pieces to the other. But neither of them could repay him, so he kindly forgave them both, canceling their debts. Who do you suppose loved him more after that?"

Simon answered, "I suppose the one for whom he canceled the larger debt."

That's right," Jesus said. [44] *Then he turned to the woman and said to Simon, "Look at this woman kneeling here. When I entered your home, you didn't offer me water to wash the dust from my feet, but she has washed them with her tears and wiped them with her hair. You didn't greet me with a kiss, but from the time I first came in, she has not stopped kissing my feet. You neglected the courtesy of olive oil to anoint my head, but she has anointed my feet with rare perfume.*

You see, this woman had made some mistakes but she didn't allow the mistakes to keep her down. Instead, she actually allowed those mistakes to influence her to act in a worshipful and helpful way in the present. Jesus said that because she realized what she had done, and how she was forgiven, she was acting in the most appropriate way. In fact, her actions were more appropriate than those of the religious crowd at the Pharisee's home.

I like Proverbs 24:26, where it says, *A just man falls down seven times, but gets up again.* It doesn't matter how many times a person stumbles; God is always willing to forgive. He will help that person to use his or her past appropriately in the present moment. The only time you should use the past is *as a tool to help you in the present.*

I enjoy gardening, and one of the tools I use is a shovel. This tool helps me do that which I enjoy. However, when I get ready to mow the grass, I don't carry my shovel around with me. If I did, it would no longer be a tool to help me; it would become a burden.

If you use your past for anything other than a motivational tool for the present, it too will cease being a tool and will become a burden.

Past guilt and condemnation are burdens, not tools. Drop them.

In like manner, the future also can be a wonderful tool to help you in the present. Consider I John 3:2–3: *Dear friends, we are already God's children, but he has not yet shown us what we will be like when Christ appears. But we do know that we will be like him, for we will see him as he really is. And all who have this eager expectation will keep themselves pure, just as he is pure.*

You see, the tool of thinking about the wonders of heaven can really motivate us to love, to be kind, to be merciful, and to be gracious, just like Jesus was on earth. In this way, the future (expectations) is a motivational tool to help you live a certain way in the present moment. "Helpful future" will always help you in the present to make plans for upcoming events. It will help you to see what needs to be organized and how to prepare. However, it will never cause you consternation, worry, stress, etc. If it does, throw it out. You don't need it.

As a matter of fact, we don't have many of the beautiful virtues that we should possess because we have not used the past and future as tools. Consider II Peter 1:4–9: *By which have been given to us exceedingly great and precious promises, that through these you may be partakers of the divine nature, having escaped the corruption that is in the world through lust. But also for this very reason, giving all diligence, add to your faith virtue, to virtue knowledge, to knowledge self-control, to self-control perseverance, to perseverance godliness, to godliness brotherly kindness, and to brotherly kindness love. For if these things are yours and abound, you will be neither barren nor unfruitful in the knowledge of our Lord Jesus Christ. For he who lacks these things is shortsighted, even to blindness, and has forgotten that he was cleansed from his old sins.*

The Bible says we don't possess the virtues like faith, self-control, perseverance, godliness, brotherly kindness, and love because *he is blind, and cannot see **afar off*** (future as a tool) and ***hath forgotten that he was purged from his old sins*** (past as a tool). So even though one should live in the present, it sometimes pays to go to the past and future in your mind, which is the only way to go to the past or future, to help you in the now.

Intense presence takes place when you realize that the present moment is the only acceptable time in which to live. In II Corinthians, Paul tells the Corinthian church, *NOW is the accepted time, behold NOW is the day of salvation.*[13] He mentions this for several reasons. The first is that the only time you can ever do anything is in the present moment. Whatever you do will always be in the present moment. You will never be able to do anything in the past or the future. Even the mention of "doing something in the past or future" brings confusion to your purpose for living and to those around you.

Let me illustrate. Recently, my wife and I celebrated our thirty-fourth wedding anniversary. I planned for the future in the present moment and reminisced about our good times in the past in the present moment. However, if that's where it stopped and I did not acknowledge the anniversary today, I would be missing the opportunity to celebrate with her now. The past and the future are not "acceptable." We need to embrace the present moment!

To get something accomplished, the past and future will never be acceptable. We are told several times in the Bible that we cannot ever get back the moment that has passed and we are warned dogmatically against taking the future for granted. James says in chapter 4, verse 14, *Whereas you don't know what shall be on the morrow. For what is your life? It is even a vapor that appears for a little while and vanishes away.* Wise Solomon also tells us *not to boast of tomorrow for you know not what a day may bring forth.* Death is no respecter of persons when it comes to time. My friend, if you would tell someone you love him, do it now! The past and future are unacceptable! If you have an act of kindness that needs to take place, do it now! The past and future are UNACCEPTABLE!

A poem I was reading the other day expresses this thought poignantly. I would like to share it with you.

Do It Now
BY BERTON BRALEY

> If with pleasure you are viewing
> any work a man is doing,
> If you like him or you love him,
> tell him now;
> Don't withhold your approbation
> till the parson makes oration
> And he lies with snowy lilies on his brow;
> No matter how you shout it
> he won't really care about it;
> He won't know how many teardrops you have shed;
> If you think some praise is due him
> now's the time to slip it to him,
> For he cannot read his tombstone when he's dead.
>
> More than fame and more than money
> is the comment kind and sunny
> And the hearty, warm approval of a friend.

For it gives to life a savor,
and it makes you stronger, braver,
And it gives you heart and spirit
to the end;
If he earns your praise - bestow it,
if you like him let him know it,
Let the words of true encouragement be said;
Do not wait till life is over
and he's underneath the clover,
For he cannot read his tombstone when he's
dead.

Chapter Three

It Will Happen

In the world you will have tribulation...[14]
--JESUS

You know, it's really not even plausible to think that you can live and not experience hard times. Yet, why is it that so many people get angry when tough times come their way? They use words like *unfair* and *this shouldn't be* and *this just isn't right*. My question is, "Why is this unfair?" or "Why shouldn't this be happening?" I find no examples in this present life or past antiquity where anyone was immune to hard times. There definitely are no examples in the Bible or any other spiritual book, for that matter. Even people in the Bible, who never had one negative thing said about them (like Joseph[15] or Daniel[16]), went through some pretty difficult times.

Joseph's brothers envied him and sold him into slavery. Joseph was eventually promoted into Potiphar's house and then Potiphar's wife lied about him, and as a result, he was thrown into prison. While in prison, he helped a couple of guys and then asked them to remember him when they got out, but they forgot him. It was twenty years before Joseph saw his brothers and father again!

Daniel fared just as poorly. Because some people were jealous of Daniel, they asked the king to make a decree that would implicate him and consequently, Daniel was thrown into a lion's den.

Life happens! People envy you, become jealous of you, lie about you, gossip about you, and unjustly accuse you. It's just part of life.

Life happens! Traffic jams occur, people drive slowly, we wait in long lines at the store, and all are just part of life!

Life happens! Gas prices go up and down, stock markets go up and down, jobs come and go, and taxes go up. It's just part of life!

If that's not bad enough, there are things that happen over which no one has control. It may not be cancer for you but may be a heart attack. It may not be an automobile accident for you but may be a tsunami. It may not be a fire, but may be a tornado. The point is this: life happens to all of us. Accept that.

You do not have to be *waiting* for these things to happen; yet, don't be surprised when they do. You will never have joy and peace unless you come to the realization that "bad" things do happen to "good" people!

When we get hurt, many times, we hurt those around us whom we love the most. Someone has rightfully said, "People who are hurting, hurt others."

A few years ago, before my awakening, I was pastoring a church where the congregation grew from sixty-five to over 300. I really felt that our church would be a light that God would use in our small community to reach others. Everything was going well. We had a couple of well-attended meetings at the local football field on Sunday mornings. People came and were blessed. Then something happened within the church that changed everything. I knew then that God wasn't going to use that church while I was there to be that "lighthouse" of my expectations. I became very angry because I was doing "God's work."

"This shouldn't have happened," I said. "This wasn't right," I thought. I then proceeded to lose my joy and peace and caused everyone around me to endure my bitterness. That is what happens much of the time. When we get hurt, many times, we hurt those around us whom we love the most. This wouldn't happen now that I have experienced the awakening. I now know that it's impossible to understand God and what he wants. I also realize that just because something bad happens doesn't mean that it wasn't supposed to happen. It *was* supposed to happen. Like the "good" things in life, the "bad" things come too.

I have learned not to classify happenings as "good" or "bad" anymore. As a matter of fact, I have learned that I don't know for sure what is good and what is bad. Neither do you. I have seen some of the "good" things in life turn into some tragic events. I have also seen some "horrific" events turn out to be the best thing that has happened to a person.

So, how about just leaving the "good" and "bad" labeling up to the only person who really knows —God!

Chapter Four

There Is a God

You believe in a God. You do well. The devils also believe in a God and tremble.
-- JAMES 2:19

A few years ago, a man attended our church periodically to pacify his family. He wasn't happy to be there. You could see it written all over his face. He wasn't much of a believer in God and it definitely showed. However, the Christmas Eve service and the Easter service were important to his family, so he came to church on those occasions. After a while, this man developed cancer and the prognosis was not good. He waited for a few weeks and then as the cancer spread and worsened, he called me and asked for a meeting. As we spoke, I brought him to the point where we had to talk about God and the *afterward*. He told me that he was ready to receive Christ and believe in God. "I need somebody bigger than I am," he explained.

We all need someone who is bigger than we are. As a matter of fact, there can be no true peace and joy in this world if we don't believe in someone who is bigger than everything and everybody! And this belief must make a difference in how you operate and live your life.

The quote at the beginning of this chapter by the Apostle James demonstrates the difference between merely *saying* you believe and allowing a *true* belief in God to *change* the way you function in life. James would go on to say that if you truly believe, it will make a difference in how you live your life. It can be *seen* not just *talked about*. It won't just be something that you *teach* to others but rather something that you *live* in a visible way before others.

Real peace and joy won't be something you can hide. It won't be something you will want to bury. It will be a light of beauty for the whole world to see.

That's the reason Jesus said in Matthew 5:14–16, *Ye are the light of the world. A city that is set on a hill cannot be hid. Neither do men light a candle, and put it under a bushel, but on a candle-stick; and it gives light unto all that are in the house.* Then Jesus continues by saying, *Let your light shine before men, that they may see this light, and glorify your Father which is in heaven.*

You see, a person who truly has been enlightened does not want to hide his light, nor does he want to take any credit for the joy and peace he has found. Rather he wants this light to be an *opening* for others who may desire it.

Also, he wants all credit to go back to the God of the universe who gave it to him in the first place. It will be *real* and it will be *seen*.

True enlightenment takes place because someone *bigger* than you opened your eyes to it. Without this someone, there can be no true peace and joy in your life. You can talk, teach, sing, or write about peace and joy, but they will not be manifested in your life on a continual, consistent basis. If you don't have this somebody, you will focus only on *what happens to you*.

Isaiah 26:3: *Thou wilt keep him in perfect peace whose mind is stayed on thee, because he trusteth in thee.*

Here's the deal: The promise of peace comes to those who have somebody bigger to focus their minds on during difficult times. If you don't, your mind gravitates automatically towards the difficulty.

In the story of Peter walking on the water in the book of Matthew, chapter 14, Jesus could have come to the disciples when the waters were calm instead of stormy. It's just as much of a miracle for a person to walk on any kind of water, wouldn't you agree? However, Jesus made the illustration very clear. He understood the circumstances that we all have in life—the storms—and the choices we all have in life—to choose to focus on him or on the storm. At first, Peter did what a lot of us do, and he chose to focus on Jesus. It was exciting, no one else was doing it, he was the first, etc. Then, the novelty wore off. He saw the storm, the waves, and the wind, and it wasn't exciting anymore! He took his *focus* off Jesus and put it on the storm. What happened? Well, you already know. He began to sink.

Our focus must stay on the infinite, not on that which changes constantly. And the finite ALWAYS changes! People change! Finances change! The dance of life will always change! Instability is the nature of the finite.

However, the Bible says Jesus NEVER changes and if we will root ourselves in him, the infinite, instead of in the finite, we can experience stability and the peace for which we so long.

And by the way, we will always sink if our focal point is not THE ONE who is in charge of ALL circumstances in life, even the storms.

Isaiah 57:20–21: *But the wicked are like the troubled sea, when it cannot rest, whose waters cast up mire and dirt. There is no peace saith my God, to the wicked.*

You can work your way around many small problems. There will come a day, though, when a bigger problem will make its way into your life. It's not a matter of if but when. When it happens, you too will cast up "mire and dirt" if there is no God in your life.

The mire and the dirt represent the physical, mental, and spiritual illnesses that come to a person who is always in turmoil. It is a documented medical fact that all sorts of physical and mental illnesses develop in people who worry, fret, lose sleep, and are in constant consternation. The Bible says they "cannot rest." Why? They have no One to look to but themselves. They have no One "bigger than themselves."

Romans 8:28: *And we know that all things work together for good to them that love God...*

The promise is that ALL things, not SOME things, work together for GOOD— for those who love God. Even though everything does work together for good for all, there is no peace for those who don't have God. They won't recognize it as *good*.

The great thing about having God is realizing that only God can know what is truly good for you. And only God can be in control of all circumstances in your life. There is great joy and peace in knowing that someone is looking out for you who really does care about you.

Fear of the future is often a huge hurdle in a person's life. What will happen tomorrow? What will happen next week, next year, when I retire, etc.? In Paul's second letter to Timothy, chapter 1 and verse 7, he says, *God hasn't given us the spirit of fear, but of power and of love and of a sound mind.* This statement about joy and peace is very important to us for several reasons.

First of all, you have to ask yourself if God didn't give me a fear of the future, then where did it come from? Is it possible I have received this "spirit of fear" from stock prices, gas prices, food prices, a doctor's prognosis, or even from my boss? Is it possible that because I have made myself a god, I think I can rearrange circumstances? You see, there won't be a whole lot of confidence in your life if you really believe that you are in control, *because down deep you know your own limitations.* No matter how well you fake it or put on an air of confidence in front of other people—no matter how many "power books" you read that say you are "in charge of your own destiny"—down deep, you know that's not true.

You know that "being in control" is nothing more than an illusion. It's delusional to think otherwise. You can't control the other car coming toward you. You don't control the beating of your heart. You don't control a cancer diagnosis. You don't control some maniac boarding a jet to use it as a bomb. No one controls tornadoes, hurricanes, typhoons, earthquakes, etc.

In high school, several of my friends died in "freak" accidents: an electrocution, an unfortunate hunting accident, and a head-on, nighttime collision with a driver who had fallen asleep at the wheel. Another guy, who ran on my cross-country team, went to bed and just never woke up. The autopsy showed nothing. The doctor said he couldn't figure it out. It was just his time to die. No one controls these things, yet someone does! The One in charge of all!

Now let's get back to what Paul tells Timothy in II Timothy 1:7, *God hasn't given you the spirit of fear.* He is insinuating that the spirit of fear is out there. But he says that *God has given you the spirit of power.* Why power? Because the God of the universe is in charge. Paul goes on to tell Timothy that God has given him the *spirit of love.* Why love? John states in his first Epistle, chapter 4:8, that *God is love.* John goes on to say, *perfect love casts out fear.* Why would you need to worry or fear the future when the God of the universe, who loves you, has everything under control? John closes this statement by saying that God has also given him the *spirit of a sound mind.* Why a sound mind? Because we don't have to second-guess, manipulate, or deny what happens. We can relax with the assurance that God loves us and is in control of each and every detail of our lives.

My friend, the events in your life are OK because God has said it's all right for them to happen. There will always be a reason for the circumstance. We are not to be afraid or try to figure it out, but to trust the only One who has allowed it. I will speak more on this subject in chapter 6.

Chapter Five

Living in the Present Moment

You don't resist change by mentally clinging to any situation. Your inner peace does not depend on it. You abide in Being—unchanging, timeless, and deathless—and you are no longer depen-dent for fulfillment or happiness on the outer world of constantly fluctuating forms.
*--*ECKHART TOLLE*, Practicing the Power of Now*

Matthew 6:25: Therefore I say unto you, Take no thought for your life...

Matthew 6:31: Therefore take no thought, saying, What shall we eat? or, What shall we drink? or, Wherewithal shall we be clothed?

Luke 9:62: *And Jesus said unto him, No man, having put his hand to the plough, and looking back, is fit for the kingdom of God.*

Ecclesiastes 7:10: *Don't long for "the good old days." This is not wise.*

Another concept in life that we are redefining is the difference between what *happens* to you and the *real* you. The real you is defined in the Bible as the *spirit* inhabiting the *shell* or the body. The real you is who Paul speaks about in Colossians 3:3 when he says, *For you died to this life* (or what happens to you) *and your real life is hidden with Christ in God.* Since your real life is not what happens to you, the present moment becomes paramount and should be honored and kept.

There is futility in not keeping the present moment. In other words, it is futile to fight against *what is.* This is not to say that if you find yourself in a circumstance that you don't like, you have no choice but to accept it. You always have the choice to try to change something if the need arises.

However, since we have already established the fact that there is someone bigger than we are, and if indeed we try to change the circumstance but it won't change, then we MUST accept it. Our only other option is to leave. Let's continue analyzing the story of Peter walking on the water with Jesus. The Bible says in Matthew 14:28, *And Peter answered him and said, Lord, if be thou, bid me to come unto thee on the water.* Now understand that the wind was already boisterous, the waves were already rough, and the ship was already being tossed before Peter asked permission to go onto the water with Jesus. Peter was *in the moment* and none of that other stuff made any difference to him. He didn't care about the wind, waves, ship, or storm. He only cared about walking out and being with Jesus. In verse 2 of the same chapter and book, it says, *And he, Jesus, said Come. And, Peter, came down out of the ship, and walked on the water, to go to Jesus.*

You see, Peter's purpose was to be with Jesus. When you touch the infinite, the circumstances around you don't seem to make any difference. But all of us are tempted to take our eyes off the infinite and put them on the storms of life.

It really doesn't matter what storm is going on around you right now, you can spiritually *walk on water* if you are willing to accept the present moment and cling to God. The only time you can cling to God is in the *present moment.* This is the importance of the present moment and the futility of not honoring the present moment. It's *all you have* in your relationship with God. You can't get to him in the past because the past is gone. You can't get to him in the future because the future doesn't exist. YOU ONLY HAVE THE PRESENT MOMENT!

Storms come in many shapes and forms. The depth of God in the present moment transcends them all.

Lamentations 3:22–23: *"The faithful love of the Lord never ends! His mercies never cease. Great is His faithfulness; His mercies begin afresh each morning."*

Now consider this. In verse 30 of chapter 14 in Matthew, the Bible says, *But when he saw the wind boisterous...*Peter took his eyes off the present moment that he'd so readily embraced when he first got out of the boat. He saw Jesus walking on the water, and nothing else mattered.

The wind represents the storms of life that cause us to fear, worry, be anxious, lose sleep, and get depressed. Jesus represents the stability, soundness, and the simplicity of life.

We have to get to the place in our lives where embracing God, in the only place we can, the *present moment*, is the greatest thing that matters in our lives. We get into trouble when we take our eyes off God during the storm and we feel like we can work things out instead of simply trusting him, seeking him, and understanding that this *somebody* is still at work— no matter what else is going on.

∫

You see, we are promised that what we need for every situation will come to us—when we need it. Not before and not after. God is always in charge and he will never put us in a situation that he cannot take care of.

∫

This is why Solomon wrote in one of his Proverbs that we are to *trust in the Lord with all of our hearts and lean not unto our own understanding.*[17] By that, he meant our own way of working things out. Instead, we are to *acknowledge Him in all of our ways.*[18] Not just when we feel like it or when things are going the way we think they should. *All of our ways* includes the stormy times of life too. The times of rough waters. The times of boisterous winds. The times when things don't and won't make any kind of sense to us. The promise is that *then he will direct our paths.*

As the Lord asked Peter in verse 31, *Why did you doubt*, he wants to know why we doubt too. I think he wants to know where we imagine he has gone during our difficult times.

There is another story in the Bible about Jesus sleeping in the boat as he and his disciples were crossing the lake.[19] The storm came, and the disciples panicked. They woke up Jesus and said, *Lord, don't you even care that we are going to perish?* Jesus rebukes the sea and then looks at them and asks, *Can't you trust me? Where is your faith?* I can almost hear him saying to me sometimes, "Hey Jim, do you only trust me when the water is smooth? Can you only trust me when times are good? Didn't I tell you that I would never leave you or forsake you?"

We are promised that we will have his great mercy and his great grace when we need it. We are not promised that *bad* things won't happen to us. No matter how much we prepare for life, there are some things we can't anticipate. Those are the things that only an infinite being can allow in our lives. Proverbs 21:31 says, *The horse is prepared against the day of battle: but safety is of the Lord.*

You can prepare all you want, but when God decides that something is best, it is going to happen and it will always be for your good. So relax and trust in Him!

Whatever you need will be there for you *when* you need it. Lamentations 3:22–23 says, *The faithful love of the Lord never ends! His mercies never cease. Great is His faithfulness; His mercies begin afresh each morning.* Hebrews 4:16 states that only in his presence, when we come to him, will we find grace when we need it the most.

Every morning, in the present moment, when it is needed, is when the answer comes. That is when his mercy and his grace show up. Not the next day or the day before. In the *now;* in the present.

It is fruitless not to keep the present moment.

How many moments are wasted with nothing accomplished because we just can't accept what has happened to us? Being in the ministry, I hear it often. People say, "I'll never get over what happened to me." Or "God isn't supposed to let things like this happen." Or "If God is so loving, why did he allow this?" It is futile to have these kinds of thoughts. It did happen and there is nothing you can do to change it. The question, "Is there someone bigger than I am in charge?" must be answered over and over again. Where is the fruit in holding a grudge against God for what has happened? Where can this grudge take you and where will you end up by holding on to it? The only thing to do when life doesn't go the way you think it should is to get back up and keep going—with the joy and peace that you can have, I might add.

In his Book of Proverbs, Solomon said, *a just man falls seven times, but he gets up again.*[20] We cannot expect that everything we desire will come to us. We cannot expect that which we don't like to keep its distance. You don't have to *like* something that happened in order to accept it. You do have to accept it, though, for your joy and peace to transcend whatever happens.

It is a great step in your spiritual walk to see how futile and fruitless it is to reject the happenings that God puts into your life. So many people miss this. They are stuck in what happened. They will spend the rest of their lives here on earth MISSING the joy and the peace that is theirs, unless they become OK with whatever God does. Solomon writes in Proverbs 20:24, *The Lord directs our steps, so why try to understand everything along the way.*

Chapter Six

Accepting the Present Moment

Surrender to not knowing. Surrender to not controlling.

The other day, I was listening to a famous news reporter's interview with a pastor. The questions he posed to this pastor went something like this: "So, concerning the tsunami in Japan, is God really all powerful? If he is, why didn't he keep the tsunami from happening? He must not really care. Surely, a caring God would not allow such a tragedy to take place. Or is God very caring and loving but not all-powerful? Maybe he really does care and love people but he is unable to stop tragedies from happening. It really has to be one or another. He is loving and caring but is not all-powerful, or he is all-powerful but he really doesn't care."

I would like to suggest another option. How about having a God that no human can figure out? Isn't it possible that God—who is immeasurable, infinite, and indescribable—sits and laughs when we try to figure him out using human concepts? How about Isaiah 55:8, which states, *For my thoughts are not your thoughts, neither are your ways my ways, saith the Lord. For as the heavens are higher than the earth, so are my ways higher than your ways, and my thoughts than your thoughts.* Or Romans 11:33–34, which concludes, *O the depth of the riches both of the wisdom and knowledge of God! how unsearchable are his judgments, and his ways past finding out! For who hath known the mind of the Lord? or who hath been his counselor?* Or Deuteronomy 29:29, which says, *The secret things belong unto the Lord our God: but those things which are revealed belong unto us and to our children for ever, that we may do all the words of this law.*

You see, the Bible is very clear in saying that there will be some things, some events, and some situations beyond our knowledge. We will just not be able to figure out WHY he has chosen to do what he does. Are we really so vain as to think that we can understand every move of Almighty God?

One of my favorite stories illustrates the futility of trying to figure out why things happen the way they do.

The Farmer's Horse [21]
AUTHOR UNKNOWN

Once there was an old man who lived in a tiny village. Although poor, he was envied by all, for he owned a beautiful white horse. Even the king coveted his treasure. A horse like this had never been seen before—such was its splendor, its majesty, its strength. People offered fabulous prices for the steed, but the old man always refused. "This horse is not a horse to me," he would tell them. "It is a person. How could you sell a person? He is a friend, not a possession. How could you sell a friend?" The man was poor and the temptation was great. But he never sold the horse. One morning he found that the horse was not in the stable. The entire village came to see him.

"You old fool," they scoffed, "we told you that someone would steal your horse. We warned you that you would be robbed. You are so poor. How could you ever hope to protect such a valuable animal? It would have been better to have sold him. You could have gotten whatever price you wanted. No amount would have been too high. Now the horse is gone, and you've been cursed with misfortune." The old man responded, "Don't speak too quickly. Say only that the horse is not in the stable. That is all we know; the rest is judgment. If I've been cursed or not, how can you know? How can you judge?"

The people contested, "Don't make us out to be fools! We may not be philosophers, but great philosophy is not needed. The simple fact that your horse is gone is a curse."

The old man spoke again. "All I know is that the stable is empty, and the horse is gone. The rest I don't know. Whether it is a curse or a blessing, I can't say. All we can see is a fragment. Who can say what will come next?" The people of the village laughed. They thought that the man was crazy. They had always thought he was fool; if he wasn't, he would have sold the horse and lived off the money. But instead, he was a poor farmer. He lived hand to mouth in the misery of poverty. Now he had proven that he was, indeed, a fool.

After fifteen days, the horse returned. He hadn't been stolen; he had run away into the forest. Not only had he returned, but he had brought a dozen wild horses with him. Once again the village people gathered around the farmer and spoke. "Old man, you were right and we were wrong. What we thought was a curse was a blessing. Please forgive us."

The man responded, "Once again, you go too far. Say only that the horse is back. State only that a dozen horses returned with him, but don't judge. How do you know if this is a blessing or not? You see only a fragment. Unless you know the whole story, how can you judge? You read only one page of a book. Can you judge the whole book? You read only one word of a phrase. Can you understand the entire phrase?

"Life is so vast, yet you judge all of life with one page or one word. All you have is a fragment! Don't say that this is a blessing. No one knows. I am content with what I know. I am not perturbed by what I don't."

"Maybe the old man is right," they said to one another. So they said little. But down deep, they knew he was wrong. They knew it was a blessing. Twelve wild horses had returned with one horse. With a little bit of work, the animals could be broken and trained and sold for much money. The old man had a son, an only son. The young man began to break the wild horses. After a few days, he fell from one of the horses and broke both legs. Once again the villagers gathered around the old man and cast their judgments.

"You were right," they said. "You proved you were right. The dozen horses were not a blessing. They were a curse. Your only son has broken his legs, and now in your old age you have no one to help you. Now you are poorer than ever."

The old man spoke again. "You people are obsessed with judging. Don't go so far. Say only that my son broke his legs. Who knows if it is a blessing or a curse? No one knows. We only have a fragment. Life comes in fragments."

It so happened that a few weeks later the country engaged in war against a neighboring country. All the young men of the village were required to join the army. Only the son of the old man was excluded, because he was injured. Once again the people gathered around the old man, crying and screaming because their sons had been taken. There was little chance that they would return. The enemy was strong, and the war would be a losing struggle. They would never see their sons again. "You were right, old man," they wept. "God knows you were right. This proves it. Your son's accident was a blessing. His legs may be broken, but at least he is with you. Our sons are gone forever."

The old man spoke again. "It is impossible to talk with you. You always draw conclusions. No one knows. Say only this: Your sons had to go to war, and mine did not. No one knows if it is a blessing or a curse. No one is wise enough to know. Only God knows."

I think we can conclude that only God understands the course that our life takes. There is so much peace and joy in surrendering the idea of having to figure everything out.

But what about control? It is really a great illusion to think that we are in control. If you think you're able to manipulate outcomes, you can kiss joy and peace good-bye. You will never have the peace that God intended.

So, let go and let God have his way. He's going to anyway, like it or not.

Chapter Seven

Holding Things Loosely

Enjoy prosperity while you can, but when hard times strike, realize that both came from God. Remember that nothing is certain in this life.[22]
--KING SOLOMON, *Ecclesiastes 7:14*

The man who *seemed* to have it all, King Solomon, warned us that life situations all pass at some point. He said that good times will come, bad times will come, and absolutely *nothing* in this life is certain. He told us in the Book of Proverbs (27:1) that we are not to boast of the next day because we don't know what the next day might bring forth. This thought in itself magnifies the importance of the present moment. It's all you are guaranteed. The proper view of life on this earth is that *nothing is certain*. Paul reiterates this important truth when he tells young Timothy that *we brought nothing into this world and it is certain we will take nothing out.*[23]

There will be no lasting joy and peace in your life until you embrace this important concept: *everything and everyone must be held loosely.*

Now, *loosely* is not the same as *carelessly.* We are not to be careless in our relationships. We are not to be poor stewards of the items God has given to us here on earth. As a matter of fact, the Bible teaches just the opposite. For husbands and wives to neglect taking care of their relationships is not *spiritual;* rather, in truth it is very *unspiritual.* It's unwise to be careless. The relationships that the Lord has given us are to be protected and nurtured. He even conveys his great love for us by telling a husband that with that same love, he should love his wife.

To hold someone or something loosely means first *that these people or things aren't the source of your joy. So when they do go away, you can still have a depth of peace and joy that is incomprehensible to most people.*

As much as I love my wife, children, and grandchildren, I have to understand that I have a very short time, at best, here on earth to enjoy them. I would very much like it if everyone in my family leaves earth in what we call "the natural order." There are people reading this who have experienced otherwise --a child or grandchild has left for heaven ahead of them.

No one wants this. Ecclesiastes 7:13 says, *consider the work of God: for who can make that straight, which he has made crooked?* If you would have victory in your life concerning joy and peace, you must keep going back to this vital point*: God lovingly cares for us and his plan is not always understood.* God never takes someone "before his time."

∫

God is in charge and even though it may seem like an accident to you, God knows no accidents. God never says, "Oops! I didn't know that was going to happen."

71

He never says, "I'm sorry. My bad. I didn't realize it would turn out that way!"

God always knows and he always cares. He loves us and wants the best for us ALL of the time. The person who will perpetually live in peace and joy will be that person who, when life happens, will be all right with it. He or she may not like it, but he or she will accept it.

∫

Again, this doesn't mean we live *carelessly*. It doesn't mean we don't prepare. It doesn't mean that we don't plan to the best of our ability. But no matter how much we plan, prepare, or care, things will happen. It won't seem fair and it will hurt sometimes. But our peace and joy comes in knowing that the person who makes things *crooked* is doing so with a full view of our lives and a complete and perfect knowledge of what is absolutely the best for us.

∫

This concept works the same way with things in our lives as it does with people. It's amazing to me that we will not say outright that things are important to us, yet we live as though they are. We need to come to grips with the fact that the way we live reveals our true priorities.

For instance, we may not *say* how important a boat is to us, but if we have to work countless extra hours and sacrifice time with loved ones and time with God so we can pay for that boat, then we are showing the priority of the boat. If in order to make payments, we allow stress to enter our lives and our peace and joy go out the back door, we are showing that things are more important to us than our true life in God. Why would we sacrifice peace and joy and love in the present moment for an object of any kind? What's the importance of that object in your life, anyway? It's not important to the real you but it is important to our egos.

There will be no lasting satisfaction in obtaining that boat, and the more time you invest in trying to get it, the more attached you will become to it. How many times have you heard this statement: "I've spent a lot of time and money on that..." You can fill in the blank.

∫

No matter how much you achieve here on earth, if you miss that inner tranquility, you will end up saying what King Solomon, one of the wealthiest men who ever walked the earth, said: "Empty! All is empty!"[24]

∫

Solomon had this to say about his accomplishments at the end of his life. Ecclesiastes 2:1–11: *I said to myself, "Come on, let's try pleasure. Let's look for the 'good things' in life." But I found that this, too, was meaningless ² So I said, "Laughter is silly. What good does it do to seek pleasure?" ³ After much thought, I decided to cheer myself with wine. And while still seeking wisdom, I clutched at foolishness. In this way, I tried to experience the only happiness most people find during their brief life in this world.⁴ I also tried to find meaning by building huge homes for myself and by planting beautiful vineyards.*

⁵ I made gardens and parks, filling them with all kinds of fruit trees. ⁶ I built reservoirs to collect the water to irrigate my many flourishing groves. ⁷ I bought slaves, both men and women, and others were born into my household. I also owned large herds and flocks, more than any of the kings who had lived in Jerusalem before me. ⁸ I collected great sums of silver and gold, the treasure of many kings and provinces. I hired wonderful singers, both men and women, and had many beautiful concubines. I had everything a man could desire! ⁹ So I became greater than all who had lived in Jerusalem before me, and my wisdom never failed me. ¹⁰ Anything I wanted, I would take. I denied myself no pleasure. I even found great pleasure in hard work, a reward for all my labors. ¹¹ But as I looked at everything I had worked so hard to accomplish, it was all so meaningless—like chasing the wind. There was nothing really worthwhile anywhere.

Relinquish your grip. It won't matter how tightly you hang on. You can't keep people or things forever, here on earth. If you try, the hurt will be all that much greater. Remember, God does ALL things well.

Letting go will mean that you can spend more time focusing on what really matters in this life.

Mark 8:36 *says, "For what shall it profit a man, if he shall gain the whole world, and lose his own soul?*

As the Bible teaches, what's the big deal if you own everything in the world but you aren't in a relationship with God?

Luke says in his Gospel, in chapter 12, verses 16–21, *that Jesus spoke a parable unto them, saying, The ground of a certain rich man brought forth plentifully: And he thought within himself, saying, What shall I do, because I have no room where to bestow my fruits? And he said, This will I do: I will pull down my barns, and build greater; and there will I bestow all my fruits and my goods. And I will say to my soul, Soul, thou hast much goods laid up for many years; take thine ease, eat, drink, and be merry. But God said unto him, Thou fool, this night thy soul shall be required of thee: then whose shall those things be, which thou hast provided? So is he that layeth up treasure for himself, and is not rich toward God.*

Being rich toward God has to be our priority, not worldly wealth and ease in this life.

Can we define *real* wealth? Wouldn't real wealth be the ability to have peace instead of constant consternation? Wouldn't it be sleeping at night instead of constantly thinking about all there is to do the next day? Having joy in spite of what the stock market does or how high gas prices go or whether or not you are popular with the "in crowd"? Wouldn't real wealth be the *abundant life* that Jesus speaks of in John 10:10? The word abundant, again, is speaking of the *depth* of life, the *richness* of life, not *more* in life. Jesus is asking what good it is to have material wealth if your soul is in constant turmoil. Is material wealth keeping people from taking their own lives? Is material wealth causing marriages to last longer? Is material wealth causing people to have peace and joy? A resounding NO is the answer! Only a life that is solidified in Christ will be the answer to man's dilemma on earth. All other means will equate to (as the Bible says) *wood, hay, and stubble*, and will not bring the peace and joy that man so desperately needs.

Chapter Eight

Identification and Labeling

*The ultimate truth of who you are is not I am
this or I am that, but I Am.*
*--ECKHART TOLLE, Oneness with All Life:
Inspirational Selections from a New Earth*

First of all, you must determine who will label
you. No one should have the privilege of labeling you except God himself. Eckhart Tolle has
said, "Ego arises when your sense of Beingness,
which is formless consciousness, gets mixed up
with form. This is the meaning of identification. This is forgetfulness of Being, the primary
error, and the illusion of absolute separateness
that turns reality into a nightmare." You must
come to the conclusion that there is no separateness between whom you are and who God
says that you are.

Secondly, you must rid yourself of all of the "baggage" or errant programming from the past. Please consider that **your body is not who you are**.

We are all going to get old and frail. If we live long enough, our health will fail because the body was not designed to last forever. But there is a part of us that was designed to exist forever. Our spirit. That is the part that we should be giving the most attention to and the part that should be emphasized while we are on earth. This part of us will never die. It is eternal.

Paul said in II Corinthians 4:16–18, *That is why we never give up. Though our bodies are dying, our spirits are being renewed every day. For our present troubles are small and won't last very long. Yet they produce for us a glory that vastly outweighs them and will last forever! So we don't look at the troubles we can see now; rather, we fix our gaze on things that cannot be seen. For the things we see now will soon be gone, but the things we cannot see will last forever.*

In a previous chapter, I spoke about Paul and Silas being in prison and their response was one of singing and rejoicing instead of complaining about the "hand" they had been dealt in life. Why could they respond in a supernatural way to this circumstance? It was because they realized that there was someone bigger who was taking care of them, and really, one way or another, it was all going to turn out all right. Life or death...I'm all right!

The worst thing that could happen to them was that their physical bodies would come to an end. That was the very worst!

When you realize that **the real you is not your physical body but your spirit,** then what happens to you becomes secondary instead of primary.

You must come to grips with the fact that we all die physically, and yet, we are eternal beings. Hebrews says, *it is appointed for each person to die* (physically). Yet Jesus, throughout his life here on earth, spoke about *never dying.* Is this not seemingly a contradiction? No, it is not. The writer of Hebrews was speaking about the body dying and going back to dust. Jesus was speaking of our spirits—that part of us that is destined to live forever. There is a wonderful peace and joy that emanates from a person who understands that going from this earth into eternity is like walking from one room to another.

A very comforting Bible passage concerning death is the story of Abraham's *giving up the ghost.* This story tells us that the real Abraham left this earth for an eternal home.

Genesis 15:8–9: *And these are the days of the years of Abraham's life which he lived, an hundred threescore and fifteen years. Then Abraham gave up the ghost, and died in a good old age, an old man, and full of years; and was gathered to his people.*

First, the word *ghost* comes from an Anglo-Saxon word that means *guest.* When the Bible says that Abraham gave up the *ghost* or *being a guest,* it was speaking of a natural occurrence that takes place in us all. The occurrence is that the *real* person is *evicted* from our bodily temple. Remember, the real you is housed on the *inside* of the shell we call the body.

Secondly, we are told that our physical bodies are just the houses in which our *real* beings live. I Corinthians 6:19 says, *What? Know ye not that your body is the temple* (house) *of the Holy Ghost.*

Thirdly, as we take time to be quiet and allow our spirit to commune with God, his Spirit assures us of this truth. Paul says in Romans 8:16, *For His Spirit joins with our spirit to affirm that we are God's children.* Go into the depth of your being and feel God. He is there! What peace and joy it brings to know this great truth!

Fourthly, Remember that when physical death takes place, this is the *opening* whereby the Spirit of God will raise you. The word *guest* applies to the Holy Spirit as well. He too is a *guest* inside of you. He has chosen not to use your body as a dwelling place forever, either. When he gets ready to leave your body, no problem. He will just take you with him! Again, consider the words of Saint Paul in Romans 8:10 and 11, *Christ lives within you so even though your bodies will die because of sin, the Spirit will give you life...The Spirit of God, who raised Jesus from the dead, lives in you. And just as God raised Christ from the dead, he will give life to your mortal bodies by his same Spirit within you.*

Just as your body is not who you are, your failures and successes are not who you are. This may include your failures or accomplishments in marriage, education, business endeavors, sports, arts, children, and possessions. Regardless of the way you have allowed your mind to identify you, you are not who your mind has told you that you are. You are who God, alone, says you are. Who knows better about who you are than your Creator? Any item, no matter what it is, would be best explained by the person who invented it. I would choose the inventor as my source of information about how that item works and what it was originally invented to do. God is our Creator. He knows better than anyone WHO we are and WHAT our purpose is on earth. We must go to the original designer and allow this Being to tell us about mankind.

∫

Recently, I visited an elderly woman in the hospital whose name can be pronounced a couple of different ways. So, I asked for her by name at the nurse's station. The nurse corrected me and used the other pronunciation of her name. After a brief visit, I asked the woman about the proper pronunciation of her name. She giggled and said, "I have been called both and I answer to both, but my parents called me——." And she told me clearly how her name was pronounced.

It was the pronunciation I had been using, not the one the nurse used. I then told her, "I will continue to say——then, because if your parents called you that, then that's what you were meant to be called."

∫

Why would we allow others to label us, give us our identification, and tell us who we are, when God tells us very clearly in his Word who we are. Here is who the Bible says that we are. I challenge you to find one negative thing God says about you!

- You are loved. *I John 3:1*
- You are a child of God. *John 1:12*
- You are Jesus's friend. *John 15:15*
- You are accepted. *Ephesians 1:6*
- You are forgiven. *Colossians 2:13*
- You are cleansed. *Revelation 1:5*
- You are redeemed. *I Peter 1:18–19*
- You are chosen by God. *Colossians 3:12*
- You are cared about by God. *I Peter 5:7*
- You are justified. *Romans 5:1*
- You are united with the Lord. *I Corinthians 6:17*
- You belong to God. *I Corinthians 6:19–20*

- You are complete right now, not "some-day." *Colossians 2:10*
- You are free from condemnation. *Romans 8:1*
- You are assured that everything will work the way it's supposed to. *Romans 8:28*
- You are a citizen of heaven. *Philippians 3:20*
- You are a branch of Jesus Christ. *John 15:15*
- You are God's temple. *I Corinthians 3:16*
- You are God's workmanship, a "poem." *Ephesians 2:10*
- You are sealed with the Holy Spirit. *Ephesians 1:13*
- You are kept by God's power. *I Peter 1:5*
- You are prosperous and successful. *Joshua 1:8; Psalm 1:3*
- You are set free from being a slave to your desires. *Romans 6:18*
- You are a light in the world. *Matthew 5:14*
- You are a new creation. *I Corinthians 5:17*
- You are clothed in righteousness. *Philippians 3:9; Isaiah 61:10*
- You are able to overcome any temptation. *I Corinthians 10:13*
- You are an overcomer. *Revelation 12:11*
- You are chosen to bear fruit. *John 15:16*
- You are what you are by God's grace. *I Corinthians 15:10*
- You are more than a conqueror. *Romans 8:37*
- You are blessed with the mind of Christ. *I Corinthians 2:16*

- Your life is hidden with Christ in God. *Colossians 3:3*
- You are peaceful. *John 14:27; 16:33*
- You are joyful. *John 16:22*
- You are loving, joyful, peaceful, longsuffering, gentle, good, faithful, meek, and temperate. *Galatians 5:22–23*

The list can go on and on. You could meditate on one of these thoughts per day and have one for each day of the month. These are labels which God, your Creator, has given to you. I would challenge you to revel in what he has to say about you. Are you tempted to bring the past into the present? Remember what your Creator says about you rather than what the accusing voices in your head say. In 2 Corinthians 10:12–13, with Jesus doing the talking, the Bible says, *Stop judging and evaluating yourself, for this is not your role. Above all, stop comparing yourself with other people. This produces feelings of pride or inferiority; sometimes a mixture of both. I lead each of my children along a path that is uniquely tailor-made for him or her. Comparing is not only wrong; it is meaningless. Don't look for affirmation in the wrong places: your own evaluations, or those of other people. The only source of real affirmation is My unconditional Love. Many believers perceive Me as an unappeasable Judge, angrily searching to find out their faults and failures. Nothing could be farther from the truth! I died for your sins, so I might clothe you in My garments of salvation. This is how I see you: radiant in My robe of righteousness. Immerse yourself in My loving Presence. Be receptive to My affirmation, which flows continually from the throne of grace.*

∫

Being conscious implies that we have choice—the choice of to whom we will listen. Stop listening to others, stop living in the past, and embrace this beautiful, present moment in which God lives and gives us our real identity.

Chapter Nine

Thankful *for* Everything? Thankful *in* Everything?

Philippians 4:4: *Rejoice in the Lord always, and again I say rejoice.*
I Thessalonians 5:18: *In everything give thanks, for this is the will of God in Christ Jesus concerning you.*

There is a story of a man who complained year after year about having to drive in congested traffic. There always seemed to be a wreck, a broken-down car, or some kind of a jam that caused traffic to go extremely slowly or even come to a stop. He would be stressed and frustrated over it. Then one day he was in a life-threatening accident, and his attitude suddenly changed. After months in the hospital, he now states, "I treasure each moment I'm stuck in traffic."

What happened? Did he become a different person? Only in attitude. He realized that every moment is a precious gift from God. You can CHOOSE to spend these moments complaining about life, or you can accept the unchangeable and be thankful for EVERYTHING.

The attributes of a contented and thankful person are many. But there is one question you can ask yourself. "Is there anything that needs to happen before I can be contented and thankful?"

"No" is the only right answer. You see, in order to be completely contented and thankful right now, you need nothing. God has already given you everything you need to be totally satisfied.

Be content with what you have; rejoice in the way things are. When you realize there is nothing lacking, the whole world belongs to you. --LAU TZU[25]

Joy is not in things; it is in us. --RICHARD WAGNER[26]

What a wonderful life I've had! I only wish I'd realized it sooner. --COLETTE[27]

The attributes of contented, satisfied, thankful people:

1. They realize that many, many things that happen are beyond their control...and they

are all right with that! Not everything has to go their way because they realize there is a Higher Power who knows and understands what is best. They realize that he sees the *big picture.*

2. They take care of business and move on. If they are "stuck in the mud," they do everything they can to get out. If they get out, fine; if not, they accept it and keep going in the best way they know how.

3. They are thankful for what they have and don't take notice of what they do not have. They know that true joy will come when they start focusing on the right things in life—when what they don't have doesn't even show up anymore.

4. They are on the lookout for blessings. They realize that every *little* thing that comes their way is a blessing. They understand that what you are looking for, you will find. Someone said, *If you want to sing, you can always find a song. If you want to complain, you will always find a wrong.*[28]

5. They vocalize their blessings to others. The Bible says in Psalm 107:2, *Let the redeemed of the Lord say so!* God blesses us every day with so much. Psalm 68:19 proclaims, *Blessed be the Lord, who daily loads us with benefits.* It's an

encouragement, and could even be a challenge to others, to hear us speak about our blessings. Maybe others haven't thought about the gifts of the rain, sunshine, snow, wind, trees, grass, food, birds, shelter, etc. The list is endless!

6. They vocalize their blessings to God, the source of all gifts, the great *I AM*. Everything and everybody exists because God has said so. We breathe because he says so. Thank him for everything! Ephesians 5:20: *Giving thanks always for all things unto God.*

> *Happiness is your nature. It is not wrong to desire it. What is wrong is seeking it outside when it is inside.* --RAMANA MAHARISHI[29]

> *All men's miseries derive from not being able to sit in a quiet room alone.*
> --BLAISE PASCAL[30]

> *The longer I live, the more I realize the impact of attitude on life. Attitude, to me, is more important than facts. It is more important than the past, than education, than money, than circumstances, than failures, than successes, than what other people think or say or do. It is more important than*

appearance, giftedness, or skill. It will make or break a company...a church...a home.

The remarkable thing is we have a choice every day regarding the attitude we will embrace for that day. We cannot change our past...we cannot change the fact that people will act in a certain way. We cannot change the inevitable. The only thing we can do is play on the one string we have, and that is our attitude...I am convinced that life is 10% what happens to me and 90% how I react to it. And so it is with you...we are in charge of our attitudes.

--CHUCK SWINDOLL[31]

Attitude keeps me going or cripples my progress. It alone fuels my fire or assaults my hope. When my attitudes are right, there is no barrier too high, no valley too deep, no dream too extreme, no challenge too great for me. --CHUCK SWINDOLL[32]

Chapter Ten

Redefining Success

*Those who have not found their true wealth,
which is the radiant joy of Being and the deep,
unshakable peace that comes with it, are beg-
gars, even if they have great material wealth.
They are looking outside for scraps of pleasure
or fulfillment, for validation, security, or love,
while they have a treasure within that not only
includes all those things but is infinitely greater
than anything the world can offer.*
--ECKHART TOLLE, *The Power of Now*

*This book of the law shall not depart out of
thy mouth; but thou shalt meditate therein
day and night, that thou mayest observe to do
according to all that is written therein: for then
thou shalt make thy way prosperous, and then
thou shalt have good success.*
--JOSHUA 1:8

A joyful person is one who has learned that everything done in "presence" *(with God in mind, and for God...my definition of presence)* is a success. Success and failure cannot be defined outside of presence. Inside presence, everything is a success. Even the life situations that the unconscious world would label as failures are successes. Nothing God does is doomed to fail. He will always succeed at his purposes. Matter of fact, the Bible clearly teaches that his purposes cannot be thwarted.

Some people are successful according to the world's standard, but we wouldn't want to trade places with them. They may live in large houses, have lots of money, and drive expensive cars, but when they lay their head on the pillow at night, they can't sleep. Peace and joy have eluded them. Why is this? They have the wrong measuring stick for success. Now let's be clear about something here. There is absolutely nothing intrinsically wrong with having lots of money or driving an expensive car or living in a big house. What is wrong is using materialism as the measuring stick for success. Not just materialism. How about popularity? Education? Social status?

You see, success has to be defined as peace and joy in the present moment. Why the present moment? As we have already concluded, IT'S ALL YOU HAVE! You can't have peace and joy in the past and you can't have peace and joy in the future. You can only have it NOW.

I mentioned earlier that anything that is done in presence is a success. The reason: presence intrinsically is success. No matter what honorable thing I do, if I am focused on God and his presence, I am successful. This will not make sense to many people because many times in this state of awareness I am not making money, or becoming more popular, or moving up in position. Instead, I am playing or reading with my grandchildren. I am helping my wife with the dishes or taking a walk with her. I am driving my daughter to one of her soccer games. I am sitting on the porch reading my Bible or just thinking about God. I am at peace! And I have great joy! And THAT is success!

If my children grow up thinking that my success is based on what I've done in this life, then I have not portrayed the right picture of success. Love and peace and joy do not come from doing. They come from Being, from God.

In the past thirty-five years of ministry, I have seen more people come to know God and the peace and joy that he gives through what the world system would call *failure* than I have through what the world would call *success*. Matter of fact, adversity has been the catalyst behind biblical success and a walk with God many more times than prosperity has been. I have seen people with the world's prosperity walk away from God, and when they do, they walk away from a wonderful and abundant life of love, joy, and peace.

I've seen failure, bankruptcy, divorce, or sickness drive people into the arms of a loving God and thus into a life of great peace and joy. Later they thank God for their failure and are grateful for all of their hard times. On the other hand, I've seen people curse the day they were married or landed a "fantastic new job." Recently, I heard of someone who cursed the day she won the lottery! She didn't find peace and joy. Matter of fact, she found hurt, misery, and pain!

There are many people who, with God, eventually found success in their "failure" and went on to help others who felt as though they were failures. I think you'll probably recognize most of these people.

> *"Failure is only the opportunity to begin again, only this time more wisely."*
> --HENRY FORD[33]

> *"I have not failed. I've just found 10,000 ways that won't work."*
> --THOMAS ALVA EDISON[34]

> *"All my successes have been built on my failures."*
> --BENJAMIN DISRAELI[35]

> *"Success is the ability to go from failure to failure without losing your enthusiasm."*
> --SIR WINSTON CHURCHILL[36]

> *"There is no failure except in no longer trying."*
> --ELBERT HUBBARD[37]

The Book of Proverbs says that *a just man will fall down seven times but he keeps getting back up again.*[38] Failure and success have to be defined in the eyes of God and no one else. Presence with him is always success no matter what you are doing. Doing, without him is always failure.

∫

It is just simple math. God + Nothing = Everything. Everything – God = Nothing!

∫

I challenge you to look at success through God's eyes. He speaks of success in his Word. It's always defined as *being* or *doing* in his presence.

Chapter Eleven

Follow Him

*Focus your attention on the Now and tell me
what problem you have at this moment.*
--ECKHART TOLLE, *The Power of Now*

In this chapter, I actually want you to see what happens when we decide *not* to live in the present moment. A couple of crucial, life-changing stories in the Bible illustrate very clearly the importance of staying focused on the now.

I have already mentioned the story of Peter and Jesus walking on the water. What a beautiful illustration of what happens when we decide to follow and obey God.

Matthew 14:23–31:

*And when he had sent the multitudes
away, he went up into a mountain apart to*

pray: and when the evening was come, he was there alone. But the ship was now in the midst of the sea, tossed with waves: for the wind was contrary. And in the fourth watch of the night Jesus went unto them, walking on the sea. And when the disciples saw him walking on the sea, they were troubled, saying, It is a spirit; and they cried out for fear. But straightway Jesus spake unto them, saying, Be of good cheer; it is I; be not afraid. And Peter answered him and said, Lord, if it be thou, bid me come unto thee on the water. And he said, Come. And when Peter was come down out of the ship, he walked on the water, to go to Jesus. But when he saw the wind boisterous, he was afraid; and beginning to sink, he cried, saying, Lord, save me. And immediately Jesus stretched forth his hand, and caught him, and said unto him, O thou of little faith, wherefore didst thou doubt?

The present moment equals God, the only place in which you'll find him. Thinking about God equals pureness of thought (Phil. 4:8). Pureness of thought equals confidence—not in yourself, but in someone more powerful than yourself during storms (II Tim. 1:7). And that equals peace (Is. 26:3), which equals joy (Ps. 16:11).

So watch the progression. Peter, in the present moment, enjoys Jesus's presence. He had purity of thought as he got out of the boat or he probably wouldn't have gotten out. I know I wouldn't have. People who are not practicing *presence* would not have gotten out of the boat because instead of listening to Jesus and watching him, they would have been watching the storm. So Peter gets out of the boat without a second thought and starts walking on water. Wow! What a focus on God! But every person has the ability to succumb to fear or anxiety, even one who is practicing presence. All you have to do to let this happen is to take your eyes off the present moment—off God. The peace (and absence of fear) that Peter enjoyed while basking in God dissipated when he became unconscious of God and was no longer present in the moment.

Fear will cause you to sink. Fear has to do with the future. It has to do with what *might* happen, never with what *is* happening. What is happening is that Peter is walking on water! Peace is happening! Joy is happening! Victory is happening!

Why? Peter at first chose not to look at life situations (the storm), which had been happening from the beginning. Because of his intense presence, he was able to excel. However, the moment Peter took his eyes off Jesus, off the present moment, he left presence and thus his fear took over.

You see, when you focus on the *now*, you really do find that there are no problems. When you decide to take your focus off the *now* and put it on the imaginary future, or in some cases, the imaginary past, you start becoming fearful. You start to sink.

∫

The moral of this story is that there are no life situations that should cause you to take your eyes off the present moment. Again, the present moment—NOW—is the only time you can focus on God. If you lose the focus of this moment, your mind can only go one of two places: to the past or to the future. Either one will cause you to sink. Only in the present moment can you walk on water and have a victorious life of peace and joy.

Another important story is found in John 21:19–23: *This spake he, signifying by what death he should glorify God. And when he had spoken this, he saith unto him, Follow me. Then Peter, turning about, seeth the disciple whom Jesus loved following; which also leaned on his breast at supper, and said, Lord, which is he that betrayeth thee? Peter seeing him saith to Jesus, Lord, and what shall this man do? Jesus saith unto him, If I will that he tarry till I come, what is that to thee? follow thou me. Then went this saying abroad among the brethren, that that disciple should not die: yet Jesus said not unto him, He shall not die; but, If I will that he tarry till I come, what is that to thee?*

Again we find Peter and Jesus carrying on a conversation. Peter decides to listen to what Jesus says and *follow him.* But once again, Peter loses focus. In a brief lapse, he turns from the present moment (from the now) and asks Jesus what the Apostle John is supposed to do. What follows, I find amusing because it is so much a picture of those of us in the twenty-first century who try to take care of someone else's business. Jesus tells Peter, "What I have for him to do is *my* business. You need to take care of what I have told *you* to do! Follow me!"

Here is another very important life lesson. To be present and totally in "Being" means that you are focused on the one life God has given you. Don't worry about someone else who is beyond your control. Hurt comes not only in thinking you can control circumstances, but also in thinking you can control others. Neither is our business. It is both beautiful and freeing when we realize we have the job of following God; not trying to manipulate circumstances or people to make things better for ourselves.

When our eyes wander from God and look at circumstances, we become fearful, or angry, or worried, or a host of other detrimental incarnations. When we look at others, we become envious, jealous, or a victim.

Another sad situation takes place when you start trying to take care of another's business— you start rumors. In John 21:23, the Bible says, *So the rumor spread among the community of believers that this disciple wouldn't die. But that isn't what Jesus said at all. He only said, "If I want him to remain alive until I return, what is that to you?"*

Now, there were only Jesus and Peter in this conversation. Between the two of them, who do you believe started this rumor about John not dying? Every rumor that is ever conceived begins because someone isn't watching the Lord. God is very clear in his Word that our words are to be used for uplifting and edification—not for gossip, slander, or tale bearing, and especially not for getting into other people's business and spreading rumors about them!

Stay focused on what God wants you to do and keep your eyes on him. It is quite liberating not to feel the need to take care of other people's business. Peace and joy will follow you all the days of your life.

Chapter Twelve

Your Life versus Your Life Situation

Forget about your life situation and pay attention to your life. Your life situation exists in time. Your life is now. Your life situation is mind-stuff. Your life is real.
--ECKHART TOLLE, *Practicing the Power of Now*

To contrast our life situation with our *real* life, I would like to bring out several thoughts. Many of the promises in the Bible are not for our life *situations* but for our *real* lives. Becoming able to differentiate between the two will allow you to understand the promises and to be at peace with what God does.

First of all, our real life is formless; our life situation is form (Col.3:1–3).

Paul instructs us *not* to seek those things we can see: form. He admonishes us to seek those things that we cannot see: the formless. He tells us *not* to set our affections on those things below—form, but rather on the formless—those things that are above. *Now, there is a reason for this: all form passes away* (I Corinthians 7:31; I John 2:15).

Secondly, our real life is not seen; our life situation is seen

(II Corinthians 4:16–18).

You see, our being on earth is made up of body, soul, and spirit (I Thes. 5:23). The body is obviously seen, but really, Jesus *de-emphasizes* the physical aspects of our lives. The body carries with it the five senses: smell, taste, hearing, touch, and sight. As much as we enjoy these senses, they are not to be the focus of our time here on earth. Not if we want joy and peace that can never be lost. Our souls carry with them the decision-making process of reason, also consisting of the imagination, the conscience, the memory, and affections. The Bible tells us to *guard* this part of our life diligently because out of it flows all the issues of life (Proverbs 4:23). The soul will decide which way we look for answers in life—to the flesh or to the spirit. As a matter of fact, we are told to *walk after the spirit and we will not fulfill the lust and desires of the flesh* (Galatians 5:16).

The spirit possesses the *faith* senses: faith, hope, peace, joy, gentleness, meekness, love, etc. For our outward walk (that which is seen) to go the way of joy and peace, the soul must consult with the *spiritual* senses instead of the *fleshly* senses. That which is seen will pass away—and there is definitely no security, peace, or joy in that which will not last. Jesus told us not to seek those things that are seen where *moth and rust will corrupt.*

He emphasizes this in a conversation with Peter, where Peter is telling the Lord that he'll never let him be killed. Jesus very boldly says to Peter, *Get thee behind me Satan. You savor the things that be of man and not the things that be of God.*[39]

My third point is that real life is time- less, but life situations are time bound. The reason Peter was so caught up in trying to protect Jesus's physical form was that he didn't understand that God sees our lives as timeless. So the death of the *time bound* really isn't all that important. David would say that *precious in the sight of the Lord, is the death of one of His saints.*[40] If physical life were so important to God, why would he use the word *precious* to describe the death of his children? We are all going to die in the flesh one way or another. There is no way that *flesh and blood will inherit the Kingdom of God.*[41] The Bible also states that *it is appointed for mankind to die.[42]* So with that said, why emphasize that which God says we shouldn't? Why not emphasize instead that which cannot be seen, that which is formless, that which is timeless?

Fourthly, my real life is about living, while my life situation is about making a living. Jesus asks a very pertinent question in the Matthew 6:25. *Is not life more than meat, and the body than raiment?* This is in connection with the concept of worrying about the future. Jesus previously said, *Take no thought for your life,* (situation) *what ye shall eat, or what ye shall drink; nor yet for your body.* In Luke 12:15, he states, *Beware! Guard against every kind of greed. Life is not measured by how much you own.*

I am convinced that a lot of people have not grasped this concept. We sacrifice so much to gain more and more. We sacrifice that which is eternal on the altar of the temporary.

It seems like we have gotten ourselves to the point where, in order to have what we feel we need, we will forfeit family time, church time, and "God time." We work extra hours to make payments on things that will be gone in a few years.

A big part of what we think we need, we really don't. Someone else has a toy and it looks great so we feel as though we have to have it. Someone else went on a nice cruise so we feel as though we deserve a break too—even if we have to borrow money in order to get it! Right here would be a good time to interject the thought that if you don't have the money for something, wait! But then ask yourself, "Is this something I really need or is there another motive involved in my decision?" Be honest! Do you really need it? Is it worth giving up family time, etc. in order to work all the overtime it will take to have this?

Even when we say we are working extra hours to buy food and clothing, many times we have already purchased something extra that is causing us to deceive ourselves into thinking we need this money for necessities. Are you making payments on a "buy now, pay forever" item? Whatever it takes, assume responsibility for your life situation to the point that your *real life* is the major component and your *life situation* is secondary. Making a living will never be as important as your real life.

Point Five: life is abundant and steady, while life situations fluctuate constantly.

Jesus said in John 10:10, *The thief comes but to steal, and to kill, and to destroy. I am come that you might have life and have it more abundantly.*

My friend, in life situations, there will always be plenty of people and circumstances that will play havoc with you. As we have already seen, life intrinsically brings change, adverse circumstances, and disagreeable people. No matter what *happens*, the steadiness of your life is there, but many times, you must practice *extreme presence* in order to find that stability. In Hebrews 12:26–28, the Apostle Paul says that God will *shake* all of creation so that only those things that are *unshakable* will remain. He goes on to say that *since we are receiving a kingdom that is unshakable, let us be thankful.* You see, all of our life situations are subject to *being shaken*. There's nothing we can do about that. Matter of a fact, many times God allows our life situations to be shaken so we will take our eyes off the life situations and put them on that which cannot be shaken, our real lives. According to the Bible, our real lives are *unshakable*!

What a wonderful thought: No matter what storm is shaking my life situation, my life can never be shaken. We must see the importance of emphasizing our lives and not the situations.

An illustration I alluded to earlier expresses this sentiment. When we speak of our life as a *deep lake,*[43] all parts of this lake represent us. Sometimes on the surface there are storms, but underneath the surface is always a peace that is our *real life.* Go down today and experience this deep lake. See if this isn't true the next time a storm comes your way. See if it isn't as the Apostle Paul admonishes us to do in Philippians 3:1, *Whatever happens, my dear brothers and sisters, rejoice in the Lord.* No matter what happens on the surface, go down deep and experience the joy and peace that passes all understanding.

Finally, ***our real life has no identity but that which we find in Christ, while our life situation is loaded with identity.*** If we are bent on being a victim, we can always derive an identity from others or from our past. Victim identity is when we believe that the past is more powerful than the present. Our identity in this mode is given to us by what has happened to us or by what people have said about us. Matter of fact, without others tagging us with identity and our own thoughts burdening us with identity from the past, we can't be the victims we want to be!

In Christ, there is no victim identity. Paul says in Ephesians 4:30, *And do not bring sorrow to God's Holy Spirit by the way you live. Remember, He has identified his own.* How can you be a victim when you have the identity of being one of God's children? That would surely be a slam to God! It would be suggesting that he doesn't quite have things under control or that he is someone who can't quite take care of his own, and thus we must make up for it by making excuses for him! You can hear it now, "Well, God didn't do a good job of taking care of me because I was abused as a child." Or "God didn't watch over my health, so now I have cancer." Or "Well, God didn't do a good job of protecting my possessions, thus I lost it all in that tsunami!" Most of us wouldn't come right out and say that God is not taking good care of us, but that is exactly what we are implying when we are in our victim mode!

Could I challenge you to stop making excuses for God? He doesn't need them and he is in charge and has exactly EVERYTHING under control. Realize that there are no promises in God's Word concerning your life situation. Start focusing on what God says is important in your life! Let go of the martyr, poor-me complex that we have carefully nourished from our past, others, and the world's ideology.

Chapter Thirteen

To Think or Not To Think... That Is the Question!

The world we have created is a product of our thinking; it cannot be changed without changing our thinking.
--ALBERT EINSTEIN[44]

Here are some truths about thinking:
1. Eventually, we all have to think.
2. We can only think one thought at a time.
3. Thinking, not thoughts, can be controlled.

I was taught years ago that we could control our thoughts. So obviously, whenever a negative, impure, or unkind thought crossed my mind, I was discouraged. I was always wondering why I didn't have the power that other people seemed to have concerning thought.

Well, I have since learned that a thought might pop into my mind that I didn't *order* but I don't have to *follow* that thought. Following a thought is called *thinking*. And even though there are many times I cannot control what thought pops into my mind, I can control whether it will stay there, whether it will turn into thinking.

The Bible says in Philippians 4:8, *Finally, brethren, whatsoever things are true, whatsoever things are honest, whatsoever things are just, whatsoever things are pure, whatsoever things are lovely, whatsoever things are of good report; if there be any virtue, and if there be any praise, think on these things.*

We are challenged in this verse not to make the untrue, the dishonest, the unjust, the impure, the unlovely, or the bad reports into a way of thinking.

We don't have to be consternated and upset just because an unwanted thought shows up. Because they will! We can't help what crosses our eye gates sometimes! We can't control what people say to us sometimes! But we can control the following of a thought to an unhealthy practice. An old saying goes like this: *I can't keep a bird from landing on my head, but I can keep it from building a nest there!*[45]

The theme of *taking no thought* that Jesus taught in Matthew 6 is imperative for a life of joy and peace. Five different times in this chapter, Jesus said either *take no thought* or *why are you taking thought*. He is teaching us that some things are not worth thinking about. He specifically speaks of food, clothing, and stature. He's not saying that certain thoughts won't come; he is saying don't give them credence. Don't worry about them. Don't lose your joy and peace over them.

Practicing intense presence causes you not to think about anything but the moment. Not what is happening *in* the moment, but the *essence of* the moment. The essence of every moment is always sacred, always still, and always very simple. The disciples in the boat with Jesus were fearful and lost their faith because they lost the essence of the true moment. You see, the true moment was in the boat with them: God manifested in flesh. Sacredness was in the boat with them. Stillness was in the boat with them. Simplicity was in the boat with them. But the disciples could only see *what was happening*. When you can only see what is happening, you lose the sacredness, stillness, and simplicity of the moment—and then you think. Worry is thinking. Fear is thinking.

Jesus had already told them when they got into the boat, *Let's go to the other side.*[46] If Jesus has made a promise, if God's Word has said something is true—that it will happen—do we really need to think about it?

Just believe. Just trust. Give it "no thought."

Chapter Fourteen

Now Do It!

"If you need more time, you will get it.
And more pain too."
--ECKHART TOLLE, *Practicing the Power of Now*

The Commitment: I will bring nothing into my present moment from the past or future that will hinder my joy and peace (my walk with God). I will protect this moment by focusing intensely on it and allowing nothing to stay that will hurt my peace and joy (my walk with God).

My presence is in God's presence in the present moment.

God's Word assures us that our life is so intertwined with God's, that we cannot be separated from him. We know that God loves and cares so much for us. If we know that this person is all-powerful and all knowing and is in charge of the universe, how could we be void of peace and joy?

Jim Colley

Psalm 139:7–18

I can never escape from your Spirit!
I can never get away from your presence!
⁸ If I go up to heaven, you are there;
if I go down to the grave, you are there.
⁹ If I ride the wings of the morning,
if I dwell by the farthest oceans,
¹⁰ even there your hand will guide me,
and your strength will support me.
¹¹ I could ask the darkness to hide me
and the light around me to become night—
¹² but even in darkness I cannot hide from you.
To you the night shines as bright as day.
Darkness and light are the same to you.
¹³ You made all the delicate, inner parts of my
body
and knit me together in my mother's womb.
¹⁴ Thank you for making me so wonderfully
complex!
Your workmanship is marvelous—how well I
know it.
¹⁵ You watched me as I was being formed in utter
seclusion,
as I was woven together in the dark of the womb.
¹⁶ You saw me before I was born.
Every day of my life was recorded in your book.
Every moment was laid out

before a single day had passed.
[17] How precious are your thoughts about me,
O God
They cannot be numbered!
[18] I can't even count them;
they outnumber the grains of sand!
And when I wake up,
you are still with me!

Wow! How powerful it is to understand that he always knows where we are and he cares! Not only that, but the Bible on numerous occasions mentions that we are "in Christ" and Christ is "in us." How safe is that! How comforting is that! To know that in him, we have our being, our very existence!

See how many times the Bible says that *we are in God* and *God is in us.*

Acts 24:24

*And after certain days, when Felix came with his wife Drusilla, which was a Jewess, he sent for Paul, and heard him concerning the faith **in Christ**.*

Romans 3:24

*Being justified freely by his grace through the redemption that is **in Christ Jesus**:*

Romans 8:1

*There is therefore now no condemnation to them which are **in Christ Jesus**, who walk not after the flesh, but after the Spirit.*

Romans 8:2

*For the law of the Spirit of life **in Christ Jesus** hath made me free from the law of sin and death.*

Romans 8:39

*Nor height, nor depth, nor any other creature, shall be able to separate us from the love of God, which is **in Christ Jesus our Lord**.*

Romans 9:1

*I say the truth **in Christ**, I lie not, my conscience also bearing me witness in the Holy Ghost...*

Romans 12:5

*So we, being many, are one body **in Christ**, and every one members one of another.*

Romans 16:3

*Greet Priscilla and Aquila my helpers **in Christ Jesus**:*

Romans 16:7

*Salute Andronicus and Junia, my kinsmen, and my fellow prisoners, who are of note among the apostles, who also **were in Christ** before me.*

Romans 16:9

Salute Urbane, our helper **in Christ**, and Stachys my beloved.

Romans 16:

Salute Apelles approved **in Christ**. Salute them which are of Aristobulus' household.

1 Corinthians 1:2

Unto the church of God which is at Corinth, to them that are sanctified **in Christ Jesus**, called to be saints, with all that in every place call upon the name of Jesus Christ our Lord, both theirs and ours...

1 Corinthians 1:30

But of him are ye **in Christ** Jesus, who of God is made unto us wisdom, and righteousness, and sanctification, and redemption:

1 Corinthians 3:1

And I, brethren, could not speak unto you as unto spiritual, but as unto carnal, even as unto babes **in Christ**.

1 Corinthians 4:10

We are fools for Christ's sake, but ye are wise **in Christ**; we are weak, but ye are strong; ye are honourable, but we are despised.

1 Corinthians 4:15

For though ye have ten thousand instructors **in Christ**, yet have ye not many fathers: for **in Christ** Jesus I have begotten you through the gospel.

1 Corinthians 4:17

For this cause have I sent unto you Timotheus, who is my beloved son, and faithful in the Lord, who shall bring you into remembrance of my ways which be **in Christ**, as I teach everywhere in every church.

1 Corinthians 15:18

Then they also which are fallen asleep **in Christ** are perished.

1 Corinthians 15:19

If in this life only we have hope **in Christ**, we are of all men most miserable.

1 Corinthians 15:22

For as in Adam all die, even so **in Christ** shall all be made alive.

1 Corinthians 15:31

I protest by your rejoicing which I have **in Christ** Jesus our Lord, I die daily.

1 Corinthians 16:24

My love be with you all **in Christ** Jesus. Amen.

2 Corinthians 1:21

> Now he which stablisheth us with **you in Christ**, and hath anointed us, is God...

2 Corinthians 2:14

> Now thanks be unto God, which always causeth us to triumph **in Christ,** and maketh manifest the savour of his knowledge by us in every place.

2 Corinthians 2:17

> For we are not as many, which corrupt the word of God: but as of sincerity, but as of God, in the sight of God speak we **in Christ**.

Colossians 1:27

> To them God has chosen to make known among the Gentiles the glorious riches of this mystery, which is **Christ in you**, the hope of glory.

Remember, my presence is in God's presence in the present moment. This is success. Mr. Tolle says, "Don't let a mad world tell you that success is anything but a successful present moment."

You see, if you earn a million dollars or hit the winning home run in the World Series, without that deep sense of presence, the fulfillment will wear off. The key to a peace that is unspeakable and a joy that others cannot take from you is awareness and consciousness: the continual practice of keeping the PRESENCE OF GOD IN YOUR LIFE.

You know enough; now do it! Tomorrow can wait!

Epilogue: The Game Changer

There are defining moments in your life that make such an impact they can change the course of your life. Sometimes they seem very insignificant. Sometimes, they jolt you at your very foundations. You may not have asked for it, but it happened. Now, what will you do with what has happened?

In any sport there are pivotal points that transpire within the game that change the outcome. It could be an injury to a key player, an error that happened at a crucial moment, or maybe something as insignificant as a coach calling timeout at the right moment. These events that take place are called "game changers."

I remember in 2011, watching the St. Louis Cardinals and the Texas Rangers battling in Game Six of the World Series. On a couple of different occasions it seemed as if the Cardinals were doomed to lose. Game Six would have made the Rangers World Champions as they were up three games to two at the time. However, with the Cardinals down to their last strike in the ninth and also the tenth innings, the big hit, the game changers, took place. You could almost feel the momentum changing. Eventually in the eleventh inning the Cardinals won on a walk off homerun. They then went on to win game seven and the World Championship.

The game changer concerning lasting peace and joy, for me, took place the day that I realized I no longer needed to pass judgment upon people or circumstances. I could accept what happened and see people as humans loved by God no matter how ugly the situation seemed. When I stopped being judgmental, this also caused a cessation of my negative spirit. Judgmentalism and negativity always go hand in hand. A major deterrent to joy and peace is a judgmental attitude of people and events.

However, before I close this book, I want to tell you how this "game changer" came to be understood.

I was studying the word "judge" in the Bible, and I began to see something I had not noticed before. This word is used in several places and has several different meanings. Let us consider examples in Matthew 7:1 and in I Corinthians 2:15.

Matthew 7:1 says, *Judge not and you will not be judged.* I Corinthians 2:15 says, *He that is spiritual judges all things.* How could this be? Why in one verse are we told not to judge and then in an apparent contradiction we are told that if we are spiritual, we will judge all things?

A closer look at the word "judge" in these two different verses reveals a clearer meaning of the definitions but also a clearer objective to practice.

The word "judge" in Matthew 7:1 is the Greek word transliterated *krinos. Krinos* means to condemn or to pronounce judgment. This is the judgment that leads to a negative spirit and kills the joy and peace in one's life.

The word "judge" in I Corinthians 2:15 is the Greek word transliterated, *anakrinos. Anakrinos* means to discern or to evaluate. There are many times in life that we need to discern what is best for ourselves and for our family. A lack of discernment can get us in trouble as there will always be times to say yes or no based on our evaluation of a situation. This lack of discernment can hurt us and those we love. The Bible is clear in many places that we are to exercise this type of judgment.

The light turned on for me when I realized that although there will be many times I will have to discern or evaluate, there is never a time I have to condemn people or situations. I understand now that I don't have to engage in this activity that robs me of joy and peace. I can *choose* to look for the good in people and situations instead of trying to find that which is wrong or unpleasant. It is easy to find the negative in others and the downside in circumstances. The price for doing this though, I have found, is very high... and not worth it.

On the other hand, to find the good in people, to be encouraging, kind, loving, and to learn to see the good in circumstances, brings immeasurable rewards. These rewards are a joy that keeps your heart singing and a peace that allows you to sleep at night.

David prayed in Psalm 19:14, *Let the words of my mouth and the meditations of my heart be acceptable in thy sight, O Lord, my strength and my redeemer.*

Did you ever wonder why he didn't just pray for the right actions to take place? Why even pray about meditations? No one ever sees our meditations, do they? Actually they do. Because that which we choose to meditate on eventually finds its way into our actions. You see, David knew that if his meditations and his words were right, he would do what he should be doing. How can we possibly do what we should do, if in our hearts we are negative toward people or circumstances? If anger, bitterness, malice, a judgmental attitude, or prejudice has found a home in our hearts, it's no wonder that we hurt people with what we say. However, if love, kindness, patience, and acceptance make residence within us, how easy it will be to show forth the charity toward mankind that we should.

Proverbs 4:23 says, *Keep your heart with all diligence, for out of it comes the issues of life.*

Truly we need to protect and guard this very special place that houses our belief system, our heart, because our actions will flow out of what we believe. We are told in Philippians 4:8 to only think about that which is true, honest, just, pure, lovely, and has a good report with it.

In order to get rid of condemning actions, we have to get rid of condemning thoughts. In order to get rid of condemning thoughts, we need to think the thoughts we should and condemning thoughts will dissipate. If we use the six virtues of Philippians 4:8 as a filter, the condemning thoughts will be pushed right out of our heads.

This is a beautiful and peaceful life I now live, filled with joy. Once you have tasted this kind of life, you will never go back. You won't want to. I know I don't.

End Notes

Epilogue
Why I Wrote This Book
[1] Matthew 6:25
[2] Luke 9:62
[3] II Corinthians 6:2
[4] Psalm 118:24
[5] Philippians 4:4
[6] Philippians 4:7
[7] John 16:22
[8] Mahatma Gandhi: Considered by many to be the father of the Indian independence movement.

Chapter One: Redefining Your Life
[9] Philippians 4:7
[10] Philippians 4:4

Chapter Two: Literally Killing Time
[11] Ephesians 5:17
[12] Galatians 5:22–23
[13] II Corinthians 6:2

Chapter Three: It Will Happen

[14] Jesus speaking in John 16:33

[15] Joseph's life can be found in the Book of Genesis chapters 40–50.

[16] Daniel's life can be found in the Book of Daniel (Holy Bible).

Chapter Four: There Is a God

[17] Proverbs 3:5

[18] Proverbs 3:6

[19] This story is found in Matthew 8:23–27, Mark 4:36–41, and Luke 8:22–25.

[20] Proverbs 24:16

[21] The Farmer's Horse by Alan Watts, Tao: The Watercourse Way

Chapter Seven: Holding Things Loosely

[22] Ecclesiastes 7:14

[23] II Timothy 6:6

[24] King Solomon speaking in Ecclesiastes 1:2.

Chapter Nine: Thankful for Everything? Thankful in Everything?

[25] Lau Tzu, a Chinese philosopher.

[26] Richard Wagner, a German composer, theater director, polemicist, and conductor who is primarily known for his operas.

[27] Colette, surname of the French novelist and performer Sidonie-Gabrielle Colette (January 28, 1873-August 3, 1954).

²⁸ Unknown source

²⁹ Ramana Maharishi (1879–1950) is widely acknowledged to be one of the outstanding Indian gurus of modern times.

³⁰ Blaise Pascal (June 19, 1623–August 19, 1662) was a French mathematician, physicist, inventor, writer, and Christian philosopher.

³¹ Chuck Swindoll (b.1934) is an American writer and clergyman.

³² Chuck Swindoll (b.1934) is an American writer and clergyman.

Chapter Ten: Redefining Success

³³ Henry Ford (July 30, 1863–April 7, 1947) an American industrialist, was the founder of the Ford Motor Company.

³⁴ Thomas Alva Edison (February 11, 1847–October 18, 1931) was an American inventor and businessman.

³⁵ Sir Winston Churchill (November 30, 1874–January 24, 1965) was a British politician who was prime minister of the United Kingdom from 1940 to 1945.

³⁶ Sir Winston Churchill (November 30, 1874–January 24, 1965) was a British politician who was prime minister of the United Kingdom from 1940 to 1945.

³⁷ Elbert Hubbard (June 19, 1856 – May 7, 1915) was an American writer, publisher, artist, and philosopher.

³⁸ Proverbs 24:16

Chapter Twelve: Your Life versus Your Life's Situation

[39] Matthew 16:23, Mark 8:33

[40] Psalm 116:15

[41] Paul speaking about heaven in I Corinthians 15:50.

[42] Hebrews 9:27

[43] An illustration used by Eckhart Tolle in his book *Practicing the Power of Now*, New World Library, 1999.

Chapter Thirteen: To Think or Not To Think... That Is the Question

[44] Albert Einstein: (March 14, 1879–April 18, 1955) was a German-born theoretical physicist who developed the general theory of relativity.

[45] Unknown source.

[46] This story is found in Matthew 8:23–27, Mark 4:36–41, and Luke 8:22–25.

Made in the USA
San Bernardino, CA
02 December 2013